NOW YOU CAN READ...
THE BIRTH OF JESUS

STORY RETOLD BY ELAINE IFE

ILLUSTRATED BY ERIC ROWE

THOMAS NELSON PUBLISHERS · NASHVILLE · CAMDEN · NEW YORK

Copyright © 1982 by Brimax Rights, Inc.

Long ago, in a small town called Nazareth, there lived a girl named Mary. At that time, many men had forgotten about God. He decided to send His own Son to be born and grow up among the people. God's Son would teach them about His heavenly Father.

God knew that Mary loved Him, so He chose her to be the mother of His Son. He sent an angel called Gabriel to tell Mary about the baby. Mary was alone in her house when she saw the angel standing beside her. She was afraid and hid her eyes.

The angel looked
kindly at Mary and
said, "Do not be
afraid, Mary. God
has sent me to tell
you good news.
Soon you will have
a baby. It will be
a boy and His
name will be
Jesus. He will be a
holy child, for He
is the Son of God."

In the same town, a carpenter called Joseph lived. Joseph took Mary to be his wife. He wanted to take care of Mary and the baby, because he loved her.

The king of the land wanted all the people to be counted, so Mary and Joseph had to go back to the place where they were born.

It was a long way to go, so they had a little donkey for Mary to ride while Joseph walked by her side. At last, they came to an inn.

They were very tired and needed a rest. Joseph knocked at the door. The door opened and the inn-keeper said, "What do you want?"

"Have you a bed for the night, please?" asked Joseph. "My wife is very tired, for we have come a long way."

"I am very sorry," said the inn-keeper, shaking his head. "There is no room for you here. If you would like to stay in the stable with the animals, you are welcome to rest there. It is warm and dry."
"Thank you," said Joseph. "That will do very well."

They followed the inn-keeper to the
stable, and there in the night, the
baby Jesus was born.

There was nothing for the baby to wear. Mary wrapped Him in strips of cloth. There was nowhere for the baby to sleep. Joseph made Him a little bed in the place where food for the cows and donkeys was kept. It was called a manger. He put warm, dry straw in it and Mary laid the baby there to sleep.

Outside, the night was dark and cold. In the fields close to the town, some shepherds were looking after their sheep. They sat close to the fire, warming their hands and talking to each other.

Suddenly, a great light shone in the sky and an angel stood in front of them.

They were all afraid but the angel said,

"Do not be afraid, for I have come to tell you good news. Tonight, the Lord Jesus has been born. Go to Him. You will find Him in the town, wrapped in pieces of cloth and lying in a manger."

Then the sky was filled with angels who sang,

"Glory to God in heaven
Peace on earth
And joy to all men"

At once the shepherds set off for the town. They went to the place where the angel had told them they would find the baby Jesus. They took their sheep with them in case a wolf should attack them.

The shepherds knocked
at the stable door
and Joseph let them
in.

They knelt down
beside the baby
because they knew
He was very special.

Mary was glad to have the shepherds come to see her baby, the newborn king.

Then the shepherds left the stable and went into the town to let everyone know about Jesus.

Three wise men from the East had been keeping watch on the stars in the sky. They knew that a great King was to be born. They were waiting for a sign to show where to find Him.

At last, a bright star showed them the way.

They rode across many lands following the star. They thought they would find Him in a palace, but the star led them to a poor stable. They left their camels outside and going in, found Jesus lying in a manger.

At once they knew that He was the
one they had been seeking.

Each wise man had brought a present
for Jesus which was laid down
beside Him.

When they had gone, Mary thought again for a long time. Why had the shepherds and the wise men come so far to see her baby? Then she picked up Jesus and held Him close to her, thinking about what the angel had said.

All these appear in the pages of the story. Can you find them?

Mary

angel

Joseph

donkey

inn-keeper